DAUGHTERS and MOTHERS
in Alice Munro's Later Stories

Deborah Heller

WORKWOMANS PRESS
Seattle

ISBN No. 978-0-9820073-3-4

First Printing September 2009

WORKWOMANS PRESS
Seattle
www.workwomanspress.com

DAUGHTERS and MOTHERS
in Alice Munro's Later Stories

One of the pleasures of following a writer's output over time is seeing how certain situations and concerns recur and develop from book to book and story to story, sometimes apparently laid to rest, only to re-emerge in alternate forms. A recurring situation in Alice Munro's stories, inspired by her own experience, is that of a young daughter's failure, or inability, to meet the demands of a mother suffering from a progressively debilitating disease, the daughter's youthful shame at the bizarre symptoms of her mother's illness, and her subsequent guilt in later years. This painful mother-daughter drama takes various shapes in Munro's early stories. It first appears in a story in her debut collection, *The Dance of the Happy Shades*, "The Peace of Utrecht," which describes the effects of a mother's "bizarre" disease and its emotional toll on her two daughters. The drama resurfaces in three stories in Munro's third book, *Something I've Been Meaning to Tell You*. In "Winter Wind," the mother's condition is "a slowly progressive, incurable disease." In "The Ottawa Valley," for the first and only time the disease is identified as Parkinson's. In "Memorial," echoes of "The Peace of Utrecht" appear in modified form. Two daughters have tried to cope with a mother they regard as "crazy," but all we are told about this mother is that she had "cataracts on both eyes," "lay on the chesterfield," and "issued demands" that the daughters consider irrational and excessive. Then the mother "died of pneumonia after all that craziness."

A fraught mother-daughter relationship reappears in the title story of Munro's sixth book, *The Progress of Love*, but without the mother's illness. Here the narrator recalls her dead mother as suffering from "a cloud, a poison, that had touched [her] life" and refusing to satisfy her daughter's insistent demands to be forgiven—though she never says for what. The original mother-daughter drama then resurfaces virtually unchanged in "Friend of My Youth," the title story of Munro's seventh book, where a daughter-narrator, now much more mature than her predecessors in "The Peace of Utrecht, "Winter Wind," and "The Ottawa Valley," is once again grappling with guilt for her youthful rejection of an increasingly debilitated mother.[1]

"Friend of My Youth" is Munro's last story to give direct prominence to this familiar mother-daughter dynamic. However, a small number of stories in Munro's later collections—"My Mother's Dream" (*The Love of a Good Woman*, 1998), "Family Furnishings (*Hateship, Friendship, Courtship, Loveship, Marriage*, 2001), and "Soon" and "Silence" (from the trilogy of Juliet stories originally published as "Three Stories" in *The New Yorker*, then separately in *Runaway*, 2004)— echo and transform the earlier, autobiographically-inspired mother-daughter material in ingenious ways. I examine these later stories in the light of Munro's earlier

8

treatments of the mother-daughter dramas to explore how fragments of an original constellation are retained but reconfigured and set in contexts that lend them a new significance.

"My Mother's Dream" is undoubtedly the most fanciful of these stories and offers one of the finest examples of Munro's comic gifts. Unlike the daughters in "The Peace of Utrecht," "Winter Wind," and "Friend of My Youth," who, as young women, harden their hearts with almost reflexive self-protectiveness against an ailing mother's excessive and irrational demands, the narrator here is an infant daughter who actively and vociferously takes the initiative in rejecting her healthy mother, Jill, apparently without any cause. As the narrator emerges out of the womb into the world, she tells us, "I refused to take my mother's breast. I screamed blue murder." She offers no reason for her behavior, simply describing her unshakeable preference for bottle-feedings in the arms of her father's sister, her aunt Iona. Some days after her first instinctive rejection of her mother — from whom she even refuses to accept a bottle — she belatedly suggests a motive. As soon as the puffiness in Jill's hand subsides, she begins to play scales on her beloved violin, causing her infant daughter to wake abruptly with

> a waterfall of shrieks . . . unlike any cry I'd managed
> before . . . . a grief that punished the world with its
> waves full of stones, the volley of woe sent down
> from the windows of the torture chamber.

9

Only now does the narrator clarify her infant motives:

> How can I describe what music is to Jill? . . . It is . . .
> a problem . . . that she has to work out strictly and
> daringly, and that she has taken on as her responsi-
> bility in life. . . . My crying is a knife to cut out of
> her life all that isn't useful. To me.

Who *is* this narrator? The infant is preternaturally quick to recognize her mother's dedication to music as a rival to the mother's single-minded dedication to herself. But she could hardly have known this when Jill first offers her breast. Can the daughter have picked up this knowledge while still in her mother's womb — where she first identifies herself as "I"? Throughout Jill's pregnancy, while her husband is fighting overseas, music is paramount in Jill's life. (Her husband dies shortly before the baby is born.) Looking forward to relief from the discomforts of pregnancy, Jill

> thought of my birth as bringing something to an end
> rather than starting something. . . . She thinks that
> once I'm out I won't give her so much trouble.

Clearly, there is something fanciful in the construction of this never named, prenatal, then neonatal narrator, so knowledgeable about her own early life and yet privy to so many of her mother's intimate thoughts and experiences. Indeed, much of the story presents Jill's point of view, and the reader's sympathies are consistently enlisted on Jill's behalf.

> George made jokes when he made love; he pranced around her room when he had finished; he made rude and infantile noises. His brisk performances brought her little of the pleasure she knew from her assaults on herself.

Moreover, although Jill's consciousness and history are followed more closely than those of any one else, the point of view does not stay with Jill consistently. Without being exactly omniscient, it flits in and out of several characters' minds. And at times it seems to belong to none of the players but to hover floating above all of them.

This kind of floating overview occurs in the comic apex of the story, where the infant narrator who is the object of everyone's concern is asleep throughout the zany action. The would-be mother surrogate, aunt Iona, returns home after a night away to find the baby sleeping. In her desperate need for sleep, Jill had shaved a few grains of pain tablet into its formula the previous night, before swallowing the remainder of the tablet—plus a second one—herself. Although Iona knows nothing about the pills, seeing "the blanket pulled up right over my head" she starts screaming, *"Dead. Murderer . . . . "*

> She grabs me from the crib . . . and . . . runs screaming out of the room and into Jill's room [crying,] "You've killed my baby." . . . .Jill doesn't correct

her—she doesn't say, *Mine.* Iona holds me out ac-
cusingly to show me to Jill, but before Jill can get
any kind of a look at me, I have been snatched back.
. . . Still holding on to me [Iona] stumbles down the
stairs, bumping into [her sister] Ailsa who is on her
way up. Ailsa is almost knocked off her feet. . . .

But when Ailsa recovers, she pursues Iona downstairs, com-
manding, "Put it down." Iona holds the baby out to her sister, saying, "Look. Look." At this,

Ailsa whips her head aside. "I won't," she says.
"I won't look." . . . Now it's Ailsa screaming. She
runs to the other side of the dining room table
screaming, "Put it down. Put it down. I'm not
going to look at a corpse."

This farcical scene of the sisters by turns pursuing
and fleeing each other, running up and downstairs, then
around the dining room table, with Iona first clutching
then extending the bundled baby, is interrupted by the
appearance of Mrs. Kirkham, the senile mother-in-law,
and Dr. Shantz. Mrs. Kirkham has forgotten what the
baby is doing there and Dr. Shantz is ready to pacify the
hysterical Iona with a needle. This involves another slap-
stick episode,

an absurd scene of Iona running around, throwing
herself at the front door—Ailsa jumps to block her—
and then at the stairs, which is where Dr. Shantz gets
hold of her and straddles her, pinning her arms and
saying, "Now, now, now, Iona. Take it easy . . ."

12

Jill, "struggling up, dopily" after her lengthy pill-induced sleep, has been present throughout the scene after Iona bursts into her room. Thus the narrator could—conceivably—have heard it related by her mother at some later point. But the narrator continues with a more detached, ironic point of view than Jill could be expected to have recounted. She observes that Iona's "yells and whimpers,"

> the noises she makes, and her darting about, her efforts at escape, all seem like playacting. As if . . . she finds the effort of standing up to Ailsa and Dr. Shantz so nearly impossible that she can only try to manage it by this sort of parody.

This recalls the theatricality Munro has shown in earlier stories in recounting the more extreme actions of her characters—probably most memorably in "Royal Beatings" (*The Beggar Maid*), though theatricality is not limited to that story.

The construction of a privileged first-person infant narrator lends the story a tone of fantastical high comedy and whimsical self-mockery that encourages us to see it in a symbolic, emblematic light. The issues it engages are deeply serious. "My Mother's Dream" is a comic variation on the recurring plot of a daughter's rejection of her mother, this time presenting the situation as the child's demand for her mother's total undivided attention and love. (This demand is not really so far from the anxiety of the daughter-narrator of "The Ottawa Valley" that her mother's illness will interfere with her ability to properly fulfill her mothering role.)

By presenting so much of the story from Jill's point of view, beginning structurally with her maternal dream, then moving chronologically to her childhood assumption that "she and some violin were naturally, fatefully connected," the story prompts us to empathize with the mother and with her struggle to have a life of her own beyond her motherhood. Both Jill and her daughter are fortunate that this other life is an artistic calling rather than, as in earlier stories, a progressively debilitating disease, and that it does not interfere with Jill's fulfilling her mothering role. Still, the narrator has apparently required the episode of her own near death to realize this. She is reluctant to dismiss entirely her aunt's assumption that she is dead, and prefers to present her own continued life as an act of will.

> I think there is something to this. I don't believe that I was dead, or that I came back from the dead, but I do think that I was at a distance, from which I might or might not have come back. I think that the outcome was not certain and that will was involved. It was up to me, I mean, to go one way or the other.

This assertion is followed by her recognition that in accepting life, she is also choosing to accept a mother who has other claims on her attention beyond her motherhood.

> It was Jill. I had to settle for Jill and for what I could get from her, even if it might look like half a loaf.

Settling for her mother, moreover, is presented as the determining element in her becoming female.

> I know that the matter was decided long before I was born . . . but I believe that it was only at the moment when I decided to come back, when I gave up the fight against my mother (which must have been a fight for something like her total surrender) and when in fact I chose survival over victory (death would have been victory), that I took on my female nature.

The narrator compromises, retreating from her initial demand for absolute devotion, and opts for a model of mutuality in which she can recognize her mother as another female creature like herself who has needs of her own. She accepts that Jill is both mother and violinist; over time she recognizes that Jill is actually a *better* mother because able to practice her art: "After all, she made our living at it." The narrator's climactic acceptance of her mother and her own female nature will also make possible her later sympathetic imaginative reconstruction of the tale we are reading.

A further indication of this mutuality is the narrator' view that it was at this moment that "to some extent

Jill took on [her female nature] as well; she took on loving me, because the alternative to loving was disaster." This claim appears late in the story and leads the reader back to the dream that dramatizes the conflicts warring within Jill with which "My Mother's Dream" opens. Structurally, this dream resembles the recurring dream in "Friend of My Youth," which also opens that story and is then set aside until the end, when it is given fuller context and meaning. In "Friend of My Youth," the narrator-daughter's dream is a wish-fulfillment dream in which the long dead mother is still alive, and while

> not entirely untouched by the paralyzing disease
> that held her in its grip for a decade or more before
> her death,

is nonetheless "so much better than I remembered."[2] The dream-mother bears no resentment for her daughter's past neglect and expresses confidence in her daughter's love. The dream dramatizes this love as well as her wish to undo her irrevocable failure. It thus reveals the daughter's gnawing guilt for her inadequate response to her mother's needs while she was alive and the daughter's ambivalence toward her mother. The autobiographical inspiration behind "My Mother's Dream" is different — Munro's experience as a mother rather than as a daughter. Yet by dramatizing a mother's ambivalence to her daughter, Jill's dream can be seen as a companion piece to the narrator-daughter's dream in the earlier story.

16

Jill's opening dream occurs, as the reader discovers late in the story, during the sleep induced by the pain tablets she swallows (after shaving those few grains into her baby's formula). In this dream Jill awakens in a house, confused and alone. She looks out on the heavy snow that has fallen onto the green summer landscape during the night and senses "something was wrong." When she goes outside, the memory that

> she had left a baby out there somewhere, before the snow had fallen . . . came over her with horror. . . . Within her dream she awakened from a dream, to a knowledge of her responsibility and mistake.

The impersonal "a baby" is replaced by "her baby":

> She had left her baby out overnight, she had forgotten about it. . . . And perhaps it was not last night but . . . . a whole season or for many seasons she had left her baby out. She had been occupied in other ways.

Horror is succeeded by sorrow as Jill vividly imagines her helpless baby waiting in vain for her,

> its mother" and "its only hope . . . . She could hardly breathe for her sorrow. There would never be any room in her for anything else.

Then comes an abrupt turnabout, as the earlier dream "awakening" proves false:

What a reprieve, then, to find her baby lying in its crib.
. . . her perfectly safe and unmistakable baby. The joy
to find herself forgiven.

So sudden is this "reprieve" that it is at first un-
clear whether it is part of the dream or reveals Jill's awakening from it. The next paragraph suggests the latter:

The snow and the leafy gardens and the strange
house had all withdrawn. The only remnant of
whiteness was the blanket in the crib.

Despite "the real summer heat," and the fact that the
baby is

wearing only a diaper and a pair of plastic pants . . .
my mother, still thinking no doubt about the snow
and the cold . . . pulled the blanket up to cover the
baby's bare back and shoulders.

Unlike the opening dream in "Friend of My Youth, this
fortunate development in "My Mother's Dream"
"happens in the real world." Although roused by her
oneiric terror to check her baby in its crib, Jill,

though standing on her feet and with her eyes open, is still too
far deep in sleep in her head to wonder [that the baby is not]
demanding its first feeding of the day. . . . She pulls the blanket
up over her baby's head, ... pads back to her own room and
falls down on the bed and is again, at once, unconscious.

18

Jill's dream that her forgetfulness and neglect have caused her baby's death can be seen in several ways. Most obviously, it reveals her anxiety about the potency of the few grains of pain tablet that she had shaved into her infant's formula. There is also an echo here of one of Alice Munro's own recurring dreams, which haunted her after the death of her second daughter who had been born without functioning kidneys.[3]   Additionally, the dream of having given birth to a baby, then forgetting about it and failing to care for it, may be a wide-spread, even archetypal dream for women. (I remember having such a dream long before there was any chance I would become a mother.) Such dreams seem to reflect the enormous cultural importance of motherhood and a woman's anxiety that she will not be able to live up to its responsibilities. If the dream occurs shortly after birth, as it does in this story, it can also reflect the radical changes — physical and social — in a woman's status to which her self-image may be slow to adjust. In Jill's case, her dream clearly reflects her failure to have properly fulfilled her mothering role. Although Iona and her infant daughter have actively contributed to this failure, her dream constructs it simply as her fault and reveals her fear of a terrible punishment to follow. The reflection, "she was occupied in other ways," further suggests Jill's guilty fear that her violin and music, which she has not, in fact, been able to pursue with any success since giving birth, have led to her forgetting her baby.[4]

Freud's view that a dream is always the fulfillment of an unconscious wish suggests a further dimension. The reader is shown the desperation to which Jill's crying baby has brought her; but initially we do not see Jill's feelings about being rejected by her daughter. We have had privileged insights into Jill earlier — her feelings toward the violin, toward a teacher who encouraged her to be "normal" and "well-rounded," and toward her husband. But our first insight into her feelings about her baby comes only after the overnight departure of her sisters-in-law and Mrs. Kirkham, when Jill is left alone with her howling child. Seeking to placate the infant, Jill by turns changes its diaper, cajoles, cuddles, rocks and bounces it, all with equal lack of success. Finally, we glimpse Jill's response to her daughter's rejection:

> She sang to me the sweet words of a lullaby that were filled and trembling with her exasperation, her anger, and something that could readily define itself as loathing.
> We were monsters to each other. Jill and I.
> At last she put me down, more gently than she would have liked to do . . .

Apart from her dream, these lines are the first explicit evidence of Jill's hostility to her baby. But Jill's hostility seems tame when compared to the infant-narrator's depiction of her own behavior as virtual aggression. Her "nonstop" crying is an "assault;" she sends "a meat cleaver cry down on her [Jill's] head."

20

Jill's response to so much infant aggression remains restrained. Seeking "a space of her own, an escape within," she begins to play her violin. Alas, both the Mendelssohn and Beethoven violin concertos she had formerly mastered are now as recalcitrant to her touch as her baby. She shoves the violin and bow beneath the living-room sofa

> because she has a picture of herself smashing and wrecking them against a chair back, in a sickening dramatic display.

Jill's aggressive fantasies are limited to her violin, although the reader may sense that the violin is a surrogate for the child. Whatever hostility Jill may feel for her caterwauling infant is expressed almost exclusively by her dream, which follows this scene in the chronology we reconstruct. Set thus in its narrative context, Jill's dream and its "real world" coda of a happy dénouement dramatize a cycle of guilt, punishment, forgiveness, and redemption. With a nod toward Freud, we may now see in Jill's dream—her neglect and forgetting of her baby—a form of passive aggression, unacknowledged hostility, the dark side of her ambivalent feelings for the daughter who has displayed such unrelenting hostility to her from birth and rejected her best efforts at mothering.

Awakened for a second time by Iona's cry of "Murderer" in the agitated scene summarized earlier, Jill hears her worst fear echoed and confirmed by her sister-in-law. But secure in the memory of her earlier—if only half-conscious—brief wakening, Jill is not immediately threatened by her sister-in-law's charge.

> Jill thinks that Iona has made a mistake. Iona has got into the wrong part of the dream. That part is all over.
> The baby is all right. Jill took care of the baby. She went out and found the baby and covered it up.

Nevertheless, when Jill hears a faint cry in the midst of the commotion of the madcap scene, she has an attack of panic and rushes to its source beneath the sofa, where Iona has deposited the baby (thus inadvertently placing it alongside its rival and possible surrogate, the more actively rejected violin).

> During that short trip from the hall to the living room, Jill has remembered everything, and it seems as if her breath stops and horror crowds in at her mouth, then a flash of joy sets her life going again, when just as in the dream she comes upon a live baby.

The last phrase blurs again the demarcation between the original dream and the state of semi-wakefulness in which Jill rose to cover her baby. But this happy conclusion has occurred in the real world. Only after she puts the baby's bottle on to warm, "holding me in the crook of her arm all the time," does Jill lay her daughter down on a chair so she can retrieve and properly

22

stow away the violin, now clearly relegated to the role of second fiddle.

Because the story has been narrated by the now-grown baby, we cannot fully share Jill's surprised joy. Yet an unrealized tragic possibility hovers in the shadows and the narrator does not let us forget it:

> the sedative in my milk which knocked me out for the night and half a day . . . in a larger quantity — maybe not so much larger, at that — would have really finished me off.

This dark possibility glimpsed at the end behind the shimmering surface deepens the satisfaction provided by the tale's happy resolution. The comic lightness of tone provides a safe space in which the drama of mutual hostility and love between mother and daughter can be newly constructed in this story with empathy and understanding.

The familiar mother-daughter drama reappears in "Family Furnishings" in the collection that follows (*Hateship, Friendship, Courtship, Loveship, Marriage*). Here the drama plays a subordinate role in a structure that moves in several different directions. Again there is the daughter-narrator whose mother suffers from a progressively debilitating disease. An early passing reference to the mother's "tremor in her right arm, a stiffness in her fingers" is followed by indications of her increasing debility (the letters she wrote "as long as my mother could still manage a pen"), until, finally, the mother's

> symptoms joined together, and turned a corner, and instead of a worry and an inconvenience became her whole destiny.

Here again, the focus is on the daughter's response — her view of her "mother's deterioration" as "a unique disgrace that infected us all" and her compensatory efforts as "a furious housekeeper" in order

> to make it seem as if I lived with my parents and my brother and my sister in a normal family in an ordinary house, but the moment somebody stepped in our door and saw my mother they saw that this was not so and they pitied us. A thing I could not stand.

The familiar pattern of escape is stated without the self-justification or self-condemnation of "The Peace of Utrecht" or "Friend of My Youth":

> I won a scholarship. I didn't stay home to take care of my mother or of anything else. I went off to college.[5]

The mother-daughter drama is presented gradually, at first seeming to be mere background to what appears at the outset as the narrator's main interest, her father's dynamic, effervescent first cousin, Alfrida. As in "My Mother's Dream," "Family Furnishings" opens with a scene whose significance becomes clear only near the end of the story. On Alfrida's frequent visits during the narrator's childhood, Alfrida and the father fondly evoke their shared memory of playing together in the fields with the father's dog when the bells announcing the end of the First World War broke out pealing. After opening her story with this oft recounted vignette, the narrator moves on to describe Alfrida's lively and liberating presence in her own young life. Apparently able to live by different codes from the narrator's parents, aunts and uncles, Alfrida enables others to see things in a changed light. With Alfrida's encouragement the narrator smokes a cigarette with impunity in front of her parents, although "ordinarily, my mother would say that she did not like to see a woman smoke," and her father (in an echo of "Royal Beatings")

> had beaten me, in this very room . . . with . . . his belt, for running afoul of my mother's rules, and wounding my mother's feelings, and for answering back. Now it seemed that such beatings could occur only in another universe.

A "career girl" and a "city person," the acknowledged author of the "Round and About Town" column and ghost writer of the "Flora Simpson Housewives' Page" in the local paper, Alfrida is a figure of glamour and sophistication in the youthful narrator's eyes. Although there was hardly any idea of a general conversation [at the usual family meals], when Alfrida came it was altogether another story.

Along with appreciative compliments for the food, Alfrida makes clear that

she was really there to talk, and make other people talk, and anything you wanted to talk about— almost anything — would be fine.

But although admirably original in her "wit and style," her "zing," in the father's words, Alfrida's political views "were not really so far away from those of the uncles," and — unlike the narrator's parents — Alfrida shares the prevailing philistine outlook of the narrator's limited world. She turns

down her big mouth in a parody of consternation . . . at the books in the book case in our house . . . some of them won as school prizes by my teenaged parents,

commenting, "Bet you don't crack those very often." While the narrator's father is willing to fall

in with her comradely tone of dismissal or even contempt and to some extent [tell] a lie because he did look into them . . . when he had the time,

the narrator notes,

That was the kind of lie I hoped never to have to tell again, the contempt I hoped never to have to show, about the things that really mattered to me. And in order not to have to do that, I would pretty well have to stay clear of the people I used to know.

The narrator recognizes that Alfrida is part of the world the narrator must escape in order to become the person she wants to be. This recognition is tied to what the story seems most profoundly about: the narrator's emerging from her constricting background to become a writer. The first step toward this goal is leaving home for college. Although the college is in the city where Alfrida lives, the narrator declines several of Alfrida's dinner invitations; but at end of her second year, about to leave college and get married, she accepts a renewed invitation.

Alfrida's apartment is upstairs from a secondhand shop filled with "a lot of nondescript furniture with stacks of old dishes and utensils," a fitting preview of Alfrida's apartment, "crowded with serious furniture" and "more like the aunts' houses than I would have thought possible." Alfrida concedes apologetically that she has

"far too much stuff in here . . . [but] it's my parents' stuff. It's family furnishings, and I couldn't let them go."

The family furnishings are the outward and visible sign— the material symbol—of the life the narrator is determined to reject. Alfrida reminds the narrator once again of the aggressive philistinism of that life by her response to the narrator's description of her college courses: "You couldn't get me to read that stuff for a million dollars."

Yet if Alfrida's furnishings and persistent contempt for books confirm the narrator in her own different choices, the narrator's imaginative life will nevertheless be nourished by this visit in ways she cannot foresee. The narrator has frequently heard the "grisly" story of the death of Alfrida's mother from the burns she sustained when a lamp exploded in her hands. The narrator's mother and aunts told this story with "greasy excitement"; it "seemed to be a horrible treasure to them." But on this visit Alfrida tells the story from a different perspective. She describes her passionate childish outrage at not being allowed to see her mother and her unwillingness to accept her aunt's — the narrator's grandmother's — claim,

> "You would not want to see her, if you knew what she looks like now. You wouldn't want to remember her this way."
> But you know what I said? . . . I said, "But she would want to see me. *She would want to see me.*"

The point of Alfrida's story is her own reply and her current attitude toward her childish self. For, having told her story, Alfrida "really did laugh, or make a snorting sound that was evasive and scornful," adding, "I must've thought I was a pretty big cheese, mustn't I? *She would want to see me.*"

The contemptuous self-mockery of Alfrida's account of her childish confidence that her dying mother would want to see her recalls the world of *Who Do You Think You Are?*, the original Canadian title of *The Beggar Maid*. Alfrida's words tell "a part of the story I had never heard." They have an immediate impact on the narrator:

> the minute that I heard it, something happened. It was as if a trap had snapped shut, to hold these words in my head. I did not exactly understand what use I would have for them. I only knew how they jolted me and released me, right away, to breathe a different kind of air, available only to myself,
>
> > *She would want to see me.*
>
> The story I wrote, with this in it, would not be written till years later, not until it had become quite unimportant to think about who had put the idea into my head in the first place.

This allusion to a story that has not yet been written is the first time we learn that the narrator has become a writer. Years later, her father tells her that Alfrida had been "upset" by the story. The narrator wonders whether this — and hence, she — is the cause of the chilliness between her father and Alfrida that has now replaced their earlier closeness. The narrator feels angry that Alfrida could have objected "to something that seemed now to have so little to do with her." But even as she assures her father, "It wasn't Alfrida at all . . . . It was a character," she reflects,

> as a matter of fact there was still the exploding lamp,
> the mother in her charnel wrappings, the staunch
> bereft child.

A third variant of the mother-daughter drama occurs near the end of "Family Furnishings." At her father's funeral, the narrator meets a woman, evidently a relation of Alfrida, from whom she is surprised to learn that Alfrida is still alive. The woman has placed Alfrida in a nursing home "so's I could keep an eye on her." Alfrida is now legally blind, has a serious kidney problem, and is only intermittently lucid. More startling is the woman's statement, "Alfrida was my birth mom." The woman then describes her search to discover her birth mother long after she had been adopted by "the only family she had ever known," married, and raised her own children, now grown up. She had to overcome the secrecy with which records were kept ("It was kept one hundred percent secret that she had me"), but a few years earlier she had tracked down Alfrida.

> "Just in time too. . . . it was time somebody came
> along to look after her. As much as I can."

The woman's revelations continue as she retells the story of the narrator's father and Alfrida walking home from school together on the day the bells rang out announcing the end of World War I. This scene is already familiar to the narrator, but the woman adds new details. The cousins regularly waited for each other off the main road so they could walk home together and, as boy and girl, escape teasing; and also, they were in high school at the time. Trying to synchronize her memory of this story with these new details, the narrator first responds, "I thought they were just children," and adds, "they were out playing in the fields," and then, that her father's dog was with them. The woman reaffirms that they were coming home from high school and so could hardly have been children, though she allows for the possible presence of the dog. Then she remarks,

> "I wouldn't think she'd get mixed up on what she was telling me. She was pretty good on remembering anything involved your dad."

The woman's comment imply a crucial revelation, although it is never explicitly stated. Instead, the narrator simply reflects:

> I was aware of two things. First, that my father was born in 1902, and that Alfrida was close to the same age. So it was much more likely that they were walking home from high school than that they were playing in the fields, and it was odd that I had never thought of that before.

But until the appearance of Alfrida's daughter, there was no reason for the narrator to think of that before.

The mother-daughter drama has evolved considerably since it first appeared in "The Peace of Utrecht." In "The Peace of Utrecht," an ailing mother has two daughters, one who stays and the other who leaves. In "Family Furnishings," there are three daughters, whose relations to their *different* mothers are widely divergent. Alfrida may have "yelled and yelled my fool head off that I wanted to see her," but as a child, Alfrida could not have taken care of her mother even if she had survived her burns. At a vulnerable young age both the narrator and Alfrida experience the loss of a nurturing mother, though in different ways; yet the contrast between Alfrida's eagerness to be with her suffering mother and the narrator's deliberate escape from hers is not a simple one. In the third mother-daughter drama, the narrator's half-sister (always referred to only as "the woman"), from the secure position of adulthood and a relatively full life, has actively sought out her ailing birth mother. Alfrida now needs care and her daughter is happy to look after her; but she does so by placing her in a nursing home. Her daughterly devotion is bolstered by institutional supports. The narrator's relation to her suffering mother poses greater challenges than confront the other two daughters. The three mother-daughter dramas are never explicitly set alongside one another, but simply placed in the same broad narrative space.

"Family Furnishings" does not end with the encounter of the half-sisters at their father's funeral but with a chronologically earlier scene. Following her afternoon college visit to Alfrida, the narrator walks for over an hour, stops in a drugstore for a cup of coffee, and has an epiphany in which she recognizes her calling as a writer:

> Such happiness, to be alone. To see the hot late-afternoon light on the sidewalk outside, the branches of a tree just out in leaf, throwing their skimpy shadows. To hear from the back of the shop the sounds of the ball game . . . on the radio. I did not think of the story I would make about Alfrida — not of that in particular — but of the work I wanted to do, which seemed more like grabbing something out of the air than constructing stories. The cries of the crowd came to me like big heartbeats, full of sorrows. Lovely formal-sounding waves, with their distant, almost inhuman assent and lamentation.
>
> This was what I wanted, this was what I thought I had to pay attention to, this was how I wanted my life to be.

Near the end of their conversation at their father's funeral, the woman's initial friendliness had disappeared as she offered to tell the narrator what Alfrida said about her:

> "you were smart, but you weren't ever quite as smart as you thought you were. . . . you were kind of a cold fish."

The restrained malice, or resentment, of the "illegitimate" daughter — deprived for so long of her birth mother and never having known her father — toward her "legitimate" half-sister is not hard to understand. But by the end of "Family Furnishings" we see that the qualities that led Alfrida to view the narrator as a cold fish are also those that have enabled her to place a necessary distance between herself and her past, and later, as a writer, to objectify Alfrida's tale as a story "that seemed now to have so little to do with her" — having become by then part of the "lovely formal-sounding waves, with their distant, almost inhuman assent and lamentation." In forging her identity as a writer, the narrator leaves behind *her* family furnishings; and yet, transformed, they become the subject of her art.

In Munro's various treatments of the mother-daughter drama, the point of view is most often that of the rejecting daughter. A few stories do show this drama from the mother's point of view — for example, fleetingly in "The Moons of Jupiter" (*Moons of Jupiter*), more substantially in "Save the Reaper" (*The Love of a Good Woman*), and most curiously, we have seen, in "My Mother's Dream," which offers an uneasy balance between mother and daughter, with the infant narrator presenting more of her mother's inner life than of her own.

The Juliet stories — "Chance," "Soon" and "Silence" (in the 2004 collection *Runaway*) — provide a more balanced presentation, through a third-person narration, of the mother-daughter drama: first from the daughter's point of view, and the then from the same woman's point of view as a mother, many years later. In the first two stories Juliet is the rejecting daughter; in the last, she is the rejected mother.

The three stories are unified by the motif of denial or rejection by one person of another's desire for a sign of human fellowship or love. In "Chance," the twenty-one-year-old Juliet has interrupted her Ph.D. studies in Classics to accept a temporary teaching job in Vancouver. When we first meet her she is reading E. R. Dodds' famous book, *The Greeks and the Irrational*, from which Munro cites a brief passage that refers to "an aspect of cosmic justice." Thus the reader may expect "cosmic justice" to have some bearing on the pattern of rejections that echoes through the trilogy.

Shortly after boarding the train to Vancouver in Toronto, Juliet is interrupted in her reading by a fellow-passenger. His offer to "chum around together" leads her to excuse herself to go to the observation car. Juliet has

> had the experience, for much of her life, of feeling surrounded by people who wanted to drain away her attention and her time and her soul. And usually she let them.

In rejecting the man's overtures, she achieves her "first victory of this sort," even as she recognizes it is "against the most pitiable, the saddest opponent." Just how sad becomes clear when the train is jolted to a halt; the man has committed suicide on the tracks. This event, however, proves providential, facilitating Juliet's acquaintance with Eric, a fisherman from British Columbia, who will later become her partner. Juliet's guilt about the stranger —

> "He wanted somebody worse than I *didn't* want somebody. . . . I don't look cruel. But I was."

— prompts a response from Eric that arouses the reader's expectations of dramatic irony:

> "Things will happen in your life . . . that will make this seem minor. Other things you'll be able to feel guilty about."

At the end of Juliet's teaching stint in Vancouver she impulsively visits Eric, providing a happy conclusion to "Chance."

The second story, "Soon," tells of another visit, which ends on a different note. Juliet, with her thirteen-month-old daughter, Penelope, returns to visit her parents in Ontario. She finds that her mother, Sara, who has long suffered from a bad heart, has now become a serious invalid. Sara displays none of the bizarre symptoms of earlier sick mothers in Munro's stories. Nor does she make excessive demands on her daughter. Juliet is not expected to take care of either her mother or the household, since a paid helper is in the home. Nevertheless, one can see in Sara a faint echo of earlier ailing mothers. Naked in the bath, Sara looks like "an old girl . . . who had suffered some exotic, wasting, desiccating disease," and Sara's mildly eccentric dress and behavior strike others as designed to "get attention," a phrase that evokes Munro's description in "The Ticket" (*The View from Castle Rock*) of her grandmother's view of her own mother's illness

> that went undiagnosed for so long, and was rare at my mother's age, as being somehow another show of will-fulness, another grab at attention.

The more significant echo of earlier mother-daughter dramas, however, lies in Juliet's response. Although Sara's demands are minimal, Juliet denies her mother the support and reassurance she seeks. Sara has been an unbeliever, as far as Juliet knows. But after a visit from the local minister, Sara explains to her daughter:

> "My faith isn't so simple. . . . But it's—all I can say—it's something. It's a—wonderful—*something*. When it gets really bad for me . . . I think—Soon. *Soon I'll see Juliet.*"

We do not see Juliet's response immediately, but only years later. In a flashforward at the end of the story, she reflects,

> had found no reply. Could it not have been man-aged? Why should it have been so difficult? Just to say *Yes*. To Sara it would have meant so much—to herself, surely, so little. But she had turned away, she had carried the tray to the

37

kitchen, and there she washed and dried the cups and also the glass that held grape soda. She had put everything away.

A repeat of the pattern with the man in the train, but in this instance, the reader, like the more mature Juliet, is left to ponder, why?

The older Juliet does not try to explain or excuse her earlier behavior. Yet her later self-questioning suggests a moral growth in the gap between the Juliet who fails to reply to her mother and the Juliet who appears in the last lines of the story. The reader infers that Juliet's greater maturity has brought with it a capacity for moral reflection that she was incapable of as a young woman. This development recalls the pattern of other grown-up daughters in Munro's earlier stories who look back with self-recrimination on their youthful selves. Yet unlike Juliet, these older daughters typically seek to justify their earlier rejections. In "The Peace of Utrecht," for example, where only a few years separate the daughter's departure from home and her return visit to her sister who remained to care for their sick mother, the narrator pleads for understanding, even as her adult narrative persona anguishes at the recollection of her youthful conduct. Their mother, she reflects,

> demanded our love in every way she knew, without shame or sense, as a child will. And how could we have loved her, I say desperately to myself, the resources of love we had were not enough, the demand on us was too great.

Six books later, a more mature daughter in "Friend of My Youth" describes the reaction of her younger self to her mother's pious view of a jilted woman, which

> alerted me to what seemed like a personal danger. I felt a great fog of platitudes and pieties lurking, an incontestable crippled-mother power, which could capture and choke me. I had to keep myself sharp tongued and cynical, arguing and deflating. Eventually I gave up even that recognition and opposed her in silence.

But no sooner has the narrator seemed to justify her youthful conduct than she undercuts this explanation with a harsh judgment on her earlier self: "This is a fancy way of saying that I was no comfort and poor company to her when she had almost nowhere else to turn."

Juliet's self-questioning at the end of "Soon" does not lead to any such definitive assessment of her earlier self. Instead, the last story, "Silence," focuses on Juliet's rejection by *her* daughter, Penelope. Just before her twenty-first birthday (or at the same age as Juliet at the beginning of "Chance"), Penelope sequesters herself at the Spiritual Balance Center for six months, then invites her mother to visit, but disappears before Juliet arrives. For the next five years, Juliet receives blank birthday cards on Penelope's birthday; then, silence. The rest of the story shows Juliet's attempts to understand, or at least come to terms with, her daughter's disappearance from her life. She reviews her past behavior to Penelope and to Eric.   In her relation to Eric we see an echo of Juliet's rejection of both the stranger on the train and her mother, and a reminder of Eric's prediction; she remembers how her discovery of Eric's fleeting infidelity years ago caused her to deny him the reconciliation he sought before he went off on his last, fatal fishing trip. Still, her reflections on her conduct as a mother, which give the reader an overview of Juliet's life into her early sixties, reveal a woman whose relation to her daughter may at times have been less than ideal, but who has given no real cause for Penelope's drastic estrangement.

Years pass without word from Penelope. Juliet retires from her job as a television interviewer and returns to Classical Studies. She abandons her thesis to pursue an interest in "the Greek novelists," and is "secretly drawn to devising a different ending" to a late Greek romance about the queen of Ethiopia who is separated from her daughter but has never "ceased to long for her." In Juliet's imagined version, the daughter is "really looking for" a reconciliation with her mother.

Juliet's hopeful idea is punctured when she runs into an old friend of Penelope, who tells something of her daughter's current life. The friend had seen Penelope by chance in Edmonton, where Penelope had "flown down" from "that place up north" to buy school uniforms for two of her five children. Confronted with this image of her daughter's current life, so substantial and so different from her own, Juliet fantasizes how she might explain the situation to an imagined listener:

> *My daughter went away without telling me good-bye and in fact she probably did not know . . . it was for good. Then gradually, I believe, it dawned on her how much she wanted to stay away. It is just a way that she has found to manage her life.*

Neither Juliet nor the narrator suggests any comparison between Juliet's earlier denial of Sara's implicit request in "Soon" and Penelope's much more extreme silence here; but Juliet's final reflections may prompt readers to make their own comparison. Acknowledging there is "plenty . . . [that] I've done wrong," Juliet speculates that the reason for Penelope's rejection

> *may be something not so easily dug out. Something like purity in her nature. Yes. Some fineness and strictness and purity, some rock-hard honesty in her.*

We have not been shown enough of Penelope to judge Juliet's generous supposition. If her view of her daughter reflects Juliet's current understanding of her own younger self, she does not make this comparison explicit. Her behavior to Sara remains far less understandable to the reader than that of the rejecting daughters in Munro's earlier fiction, whose suffering mothers demanded a sustained attention the daughter were unable

41

or unwilling to provide. Even though we recognize the element of retribution at work in Penelope's silence to Juliet, it is hard to see any real moral logic to this pattern. To be sure, the retributive structure may remind us of the passage in Dodds' book on Greek tragedy that Juliet was reading when we first met her:

> . . . *what to the partial vision of the living appears as the act of the fiend, is perceived by the wider insight of the dead to be an act of cosmic justice* . . .

But the world described by Dodd can offer only an ironic contrast to the contemporary world of the Juliet stories, in which claims to a transcendental spiritual order have been raised only to be dismissed. (The smugly self-confident guru of Penelope's new age Spiritual Balance Center and Sara's diabetic minister friend are hardly fig-ures to inspire faith in the higher spiritual dimension they claim to represent.) The trilogy deliberately refuses to provide a context for understanding Penelope's silence as "an act of cosmic justice." Instead, the three stories dem-onstrate a carefully constructed, ineluctable *poetic* justice, in which a daughter's rejection of her mother is no longer explained, justified, rationalized, or even condemned, as it has been in earlier stories, but is simply punished, as by some iron law of retribution.[6]

The absence of any clearly discernible motive for Penelope's silence gives this story a universal resonance. The estrangement of Munro's earlier stories, caused by a daughter's need to escape from a mother's bizarre disease, excessive demands, or rigid puritanical values, has been replaced by a situation that is more common, though no less painful—the daughter's simply choosing a life in which, for no obvious reason, she does not wish to include her mother. But viewing the rejected mother here from within, we are left with a less irrevocable, more open-ended conclusion. Unlike earlier mothers, Juliet is alive and healthy at the end of "Silence." Hence,

> She keeps on hoping for a word from Penelope, but not in any strenuous way. She hopes as people who know better hope for undeserved blessings, spontaneous remissions, things of that sort.

NOTES

[1]In a frequently cited comment about her mother, Munro says, "The first real story I ever wrote was about her" (Hancock 215). Subsequent interviews reiterate her mother's importance. Even when Munro observes, "I'm doing less personal writing now than I used to," she affirms, "The material about my mother is my central material in life, and it always comes the most readily to me" ("The Art of Fiction" 244, 237). A fuller discussion of "Friend of My Youth" in the context of Munro's earlier stories can be found in my book, *Literary Sisterhoods* (Heller 69-78). Of "Friend of My Youth" Munro has said, "It works at my deepest level" ("Art of Fiction" 241).

[2]A close echo of the opening of "Friend of My Youth" can be found in "The Ticket" in Munro's recent, frankly autobiographical collection, *The View from Castle Rock*: "Sometimes I dream about my grandmother and her sister. . . . they are still living in the house where they lived for twenty years or so. . . . I am shocked to find that they are alive and I am amazed, ashamed to think that I have not visited them" (255).

[3]Munro's second daughter, Catherine, was born and died within a day in July 1955. She told Ross that, until the birth of her third daughter, Jenny, in 1957, she "was haunted by recurring dreams. I was doing something and

45

had the feeling I was forgetting something very, very important. It was a baby. I had left it outside and forgotten about it, and it was out in the rain. By the time I remembered what it was, the baby was dead'" (Ross 53). Sheila Munro tells the same story (43).

In a TV interview with Paula Todd, Munro spoke of her recurrent dream of having left a baby "under the rain . . . for weeks," specifying that she had used this dream in her story "My Mother's Dream." Munro and her husband "were very anti-sentimental," she added, "so we just rolled with it. We didn't mention it much. It bothered me more later than it did then. . . . To refer to it much in the context of our marriage would have been self-indulgent." It was not until 1990, when she was in British Columbia for her oldest daughter's marriage, that Munro arranged for a gravestone for Catherine. By then, "I was not afraid to do something that might be seen as sentimental, false, and self-gratifying. I think when I was younger that might have been the interpretation." Thacker discusses Munro's treatments of the dead baby in poetry and unpublished drafts of stories well before "My Mother's Dream" (125-6).

[4]Munro's answer to interviewer Todd's question, "Did you feel guilt?" suggests a parallel between her own conflicts at the time and those of the fictional musician-mother she created many years later: "I must have. Maybe I felt some guilt about not being a totally motherly woman. You know, about wanting other things."

[5]In a recent interview Munro describes leaving home for university in very similar terms: "This is the thing with which I'll be able to nourish my guilt for the rest of my life — that I did not stay home. I did not look after my mother . . . I did not keep house, though my brother and sister were still quite young. I just left them" (Wachtel 278).

[6]Cosmic justice implies the existence of a wider cosmos that operates according to principles of justice, which may remain mysterious to human reason. "Poetic justice" implies no such metaphysical resonance; it refers simply to the *author's* distribution, at the end of a literary work, of earthly rewards and punishments in proportion to the virtue or vice of the various characters" (M. H. Abrams, *A Glossary of Literary Terms*). But it is still hard to see any "vice" in Juliet that deserves the drastic punishment she receives.

[7]In the context of Juliet's classical interests, her hope may represent an intriguing inversion of the situation in *The Odyssey*, where it is Penelope who is hoping and waiting (albeit for her husband). The conclusion further suggests a dramatic irony in the proleptic wish-fulfillment of Juliet's choice of her daughter's name.

WORKS CITED

Abrams, M. H. *A Glossary of Literary Terms*. 5th Edition. NY: Holt, Rinehart and Winston, Inc., 1988.

Hancock, Geoff. "Alice Munro." *Canadian Writers at Work: Interviews with Geoff Hancock*. Toronto: Oxford, 1987. 187-225.

Heller, Deborah. *Literary Sisterhoods: Imagining Women Artists*. Montreal & Kingston: McGill-Queen's University Press. 2005. 69-89

Munro, Alice. "The Art of Fiction" CXXXVII. Interview with Jeanne McCulloch, Mona Simpson. *Paris Review* 131 (1994): 227-64.

---. *Dance of the Happy Shades*. 1968. Toronto: McGraw-Hill, 1988.

---. *Hateship, Friendship, Courtship, Loveship, Marriage*. Toronto: McClelland & Stewart Ltd., 2001.

---. *Friend of My Youth*. 1990. Toronto: Penguin, 1991.

---. *The Love of a Good Woman*. Toronto: McClelland & Stewart Inc., 1998.

---. *The Moons of Jupiter*. 1982. Toronto: Penguin, 1986.

---. *The Progress of Love*. 1986. Toronto: Penguin: 1987.

---. *Runaway*. Toronto: McClelland & Stewart Ltd., 2004.

---. *Something I've Been Meaning to Tell You*. 1974. Toronto: Penguin, 1990.

---. "Three Stories: "Chance," "Soon," "Silence." *The New Yorker* 14 & 21 June 2004: 130+. (Reprinted in Munro, *Runaway* 48-159.)

---. *Who Do You Think You Are?* 1978. Toronto: Penguin, 1991.

---. *The View from Castle Rock*. Toronto: McClelland & Stewart, 2006.

Munro, Sheila. *Lives of Mothers and Daughters: Growing Up With Alice Munro*. Toronto: McClelland & Stewart, 2001.

Ross, Catherine Sheldrick. *Alice Munro: A Double Life*. Toronto: ECW Press, 1992.

Thacker, Robert. *Alice Munro: Writing Her Lives*. Toronto: McClelland & Stewart, 2005.

Todd, Paula. Interview with Alice Munro. "Person 2 Person." TVO. April 5, 2006.

Wachtel, Eleanor. "Alice Munro: A Life in Writing. A Conversation." *Queen's Quarterly* 112:2 (Summer 2005), 267-281.

LaVergne, TN USA
18 September 2009
158359LV00004B/4/P